Why God Is a Woman

Why God Is a Woman

poems by
Nin Andrews

AMERICAN POETS CONTINUUM SERIES, NO. 148

BOA EDITIONS, LTD ❧ ROCHESTER, NY ❧ 2015

First Edition
15 16 17 18 7 6 5 4 3 2 1

For information about permission to reuse any material from this book please contact The
Permissions Company at www.permissionscompany.com or e-mail permdude@eclipse.net.

Publications by BOA Editions, Ltd.—a not-for-profit corporation
under section 501 (c) (3) of the United States Internal Revenue
Code—are made possible with funds from a variety of sources,
including public funds from the New York State Council on the
Arts, a state agency; the Literature Program of the National
Endowment for the Arts; the County of Monroe, NY; the Lannan
Foundation for support of the Lannan Translations Selection
Series; the Mary S. Mulligan Charitable Trust; the Rochester Area
Community Foundation; the Arts & Cultural Council for Greater
Rochester; the Steeple-Jack Fund; the Ames-Amzalak Memorial Trust in memory of Henry
Ames, Semon Amzalak and Dan Amzalak; and contributions from many individuals nation-
wide. See Colophon on page 96 for special individual acknowledgments.

ART WORKS.
arts.gov

State of the Arts

NYSCA

Cover Design: Sandy Knight
Interior Design and Composition: Richard Foerster
Manufacturing: Versa Press, Inc.
BOA Logo: Mirko

Library of Congress Cataloging-in-Publication Data

Andrews, Nin.
[Poems. Selections]
Why god is a woman : poems / by Nin Andrews. — First edition.
    pages ; cm. — (American poets continuum series ; no. 148)
ISBN 978-1-938160-61-5 (softcover) — ISBN 978-1-938160-62-2 (ebook)
I. Title.
PS3551.N444A6 2015
811'.54—dc23

2014039640

BOA Editions, Ltd.
250 North Goodman Street, Suite 306
Rochester, NY 14607
www.boaeditions.org
A. Poulin, Jr., Founder (1938–1996)

Contents

30   **On the Island where I grew up**
    the women sat on their porches at dusk . . .

31   **On the Island where I come from**
    the men are so beautiful . . .

32   **On the Island where I come from**
    the men are written up in tourist magazines . . .

33   **On the Island where I come from**
    there are many stories about why . . .

34   **On the Island where I come from**
    casinos are especially popular . . .

35   **On the Island where I come from**
    no woman will make love to a man . . .

36   **On the Island where I come from**
    it is said that God, Herself, pines . . .

37   **On the Island where I come from**
    vagina envy is the most common . . .

38   **On the Island where I come from**
    many Island men and boys suffer . . .

39   **On the Island where I come from**
    a hardworking woman is most admired.

40   **On the Island where I come from**
    the hardworking woman is forever in search . . .

41   **On the Island where I come from**
    only women hold political office.

42   **On the Island where I come from**
    Dolly Delita is a world-famous man-trainer.

43   **On the Island where I come from**
    St. Julio's Finishing School . . .

45   **On the Island where I come from**
    Relinquishing Self was a standard lesson . . .

46   **On the Island where I come from**
    the most popular toy for boys . . .

47   **On the Island where I come from**
    both male and female children have
    mango-sized brains . . .

48   **On the Island where I grew up**
    my favorite Boberto dolls slept on my pillow . . .

49   **On the Island where I grew up**
    when I was a boy, I confided in Angelina . . .

This book is dedicated to my daughter, Suzanne,
and my dear friend, Anne Marie, two powerful women
who have inspired me to think deeply about the question,
What does it mean to be a woman?

On the Island where I come from

women rule. They run the country, control the wealth, and decide who will do what, why, and when. At the end of the day, when the sun sinks into the sea, the women leave their offices behind and go out on the town to enjoy what is known as *the women's hour.* In bars, restaurants, and spas designed for women only, they relax and let out a sigh as the day's thoughts and fears rush off their skin like water. There they linger as day fades from the sky, chatting among themselves, making occasional cracks about the guys. Men, they say, are such incomplete souls. *They don't even know how to love,* they say as they grow calm in the light of their minds before returning to their homes: their men, their children, their dogs.

On the Island where I grew up

when I was a boy, my mother would take me to *The Girls Club* after work where she would drink martinis and tell the ladies how she had so hoped for another girl. *But he's such a darling little thing*, the ladies would tisk, picking me up in their arms. Dolly, the redhead, would dance me around the room, my head crushed against her huge breasts. When she was soused, she would reach into my pants with her long fingernails, checking to see if my fruit was ripe. *Hands off, Dolly,* my mother would say, swishing me away in her arms. *He's not yours yet.* They would all laugh. Dolly had a reputation. She was our local fruit picker. Her claim to fame, she had once slept with Julio Vega, our Island beauty king. Julio Vega was the name on everyone's lips back then. *Julio Vega, Julio Vega,* the women sighed and giggled and sang. To become the next Julio Vega was every Island boy's dream.

Julio Vega

Julio Vega, Julio Vega. His name was on everyone's lips. Julio Vega was the first man on the Island to run for president. Not that the Islanders would ever elect a man to run our island-country. After all, the men had only recently won the right to vote back then. But women loved Julio Vega for his long dark eyelashes, his curly locks, and his luscious thighs, displayed in our famous ad for coconut oil on billboards and TV screens across the country.

Julio Vega was crowned our Island beauty king year after year at the fall harvest festival. Paraded around town, he was the centerpiece in a float of adoring women. Rumor had it that he was even more beautiful in person than on screen. Once a woman met Julio Vega in the skin, my mother said, she was never the same. She would hang on his every word, gesture, and glance. Julio loved the women loving him. That's why he said whatever they wanted to hear, and they nodded and clapped and cheered.

A man's place is at the feet of his woman, he announced when he was running for president. *A man is meant to do physical labor and menial jobs like paving roads, sweeping floors, and cleaning latrines, for this is the work God designed for Island men. If God had wanted men to do office work, he would have made them less muscular, less angry, less beautiful, less eager for sex and war.*

The liberal men, of course, were enraged by his words. They were overcome with jealousy of his good looks. But soon they began to dress like Julio, to wear glasses like Julio, even to buy the coconut oil and shampoo Julio Vega was said to use. In this way the men became Julio-men, and the women hummed around them like bees around blossoms before ascending to their glass offices in the sky.

On the Island where I come from

the men earned seventy cents for every dollar the women made. The women had little faith in the male work ethic. As my mother explained it, men lack patience, the key to great work. The metaphor she used: a man impregnates a woman in a single night, but he never understands the long months of swelling with child. While the Island women worked day and night, tending the Island's needs, the men worked only the daylight hours, which exhausted them so completely, they fell into a deep sleep at the end of the day, never waking to the cries of infants, birds, angels, or the youth who were partying in the streets.

This, of course, was not the men's fault. Men, my mother said, can't be blamed for their genetic defects and limited work ethic or abilities. Besides, the best men are those who are satisfied with their traditional Island roles. Yet when I was a boy, men marched in the streets, waving signs and demanding equal pay, jobs, and rights. Every few years the women gave the men a small raise. They hired a few more token men. But when the economy soured, the women stopped hiring or giving raises. They said they were only willing to pay a man what he was worth, not a penny more. The worth of a man was an ongoing Island debate.

On the Island where I come from

the men look like African parrots when they dress in their fashionable Island garb, designed to show off the body's graceful motions, the rise and fall of each breath, thigh, and biceps. Popular are the revealing blouses left unbuttoned to display the male chest and abdominal muscles and the traditional Island tattoo of a native flowering vine that begins at the navel and twines below the belt where the male flower blooms.

Some men, however, object to being seen as sex objects. They refuse to wear the latest styles. Instead they dress in the skirts and gowns that professional women wear. Walking the sidewalks, trying to balance on ladies pumps and heels, the men waddle from side to side. The locals call them penguins and toss insults and small stones when they pass by.

The men in dresses do not despair. They say it is only in dresses that they can speak with soft voices, think gentle thoughts, and be respected and heard. Only in dresses can they visit the women's salons and clubs and share in the gossip and important news of the town. Only in dresses can they enter the intimate realm of feminine mystique, power, and politics that run our Island.

On the Island where I come from

the women laugh when they talk of the men who dress in women's skirts and gowns. *Do these men really think they should earn as much as women? Maybe then they will enjoy multiple orgasms, too. And no longer need to apologize at the end of the day: I am so sorry, Honey, I have a headache.*

Of course, they know this will never happen. Men will never be as capable as women. As Aristea, the great Island philosopher, pointed out centuries ago, men are simply unfinished ladies. *No wonder they feel inferior,* the women smirk. Island women, on the other hand, know that just as the sea reflects the heavens, women reflect the divine. For only women are made in God's own image and likeness.

The Token Man

Placing a cup of steaming coffee on the boss's desk, the token man listens to her prattle on and on with her assistant. *Would you like a croissant or a donut, Miss Angelina?* he asks, as if he were merely her secretary. *No*, his boss says, barely acknowledging him or pausing mid-sentence. He watches her in the large mirror that hangs on the office wall as she opens and closes her mouth like a fish in a tank. Only a fish makes no noise, he thinks. When she looks up expectantly, he clears the coffee cups away and takes out the garbage. He feels his boss watching his every move. *It's always like this*, he sighs. The powerful women check out the young men's asses, thighs, quads. (His are toned and outlined in his Lycra red pantsuit. That's probably why she hired him, he knows. How he hates Lycra, the fabric meant to humiliate men.) And he hates it when they ask when he's going to get married and have a family. Of course, he will have to quit work and raise children then. Isn't that what everyone expects? But his boss is happy he's a bachelor. She's always winking at him and saying how grateful he should be, having a job in the city, living in the high-rent district, eating lunches with her in clubs and fancy bars and restaurants where men were only recently allowed to enter, much less dine.

On the Island where I come from

numerous articles were written about men in the workplace. Island social scientists concluded that the hiring of men was nothing more than a failed experiment. Why? Because biology is destiny. Island men are designed for domesticity. Scientists often quoted the working men who admitted their inability to repress their instinctive natures, i.e., a profound longing to have, hold, and nurture their own children. But one father suggested philosophically, *Perhaps all Islanders, regardless of gender, sit by the window when darkness falls and dream of something else.*

problems occur when Island men are hired to work alongside women. For the Island men, unlike the Island women, lack self-control. In fits of anger, the men turn offices into chicken coops with upturned papers, coffee cups, and feathers flying everywhere. In moments of joy, they open bottles of champagne, spread their wings, and leap from office windows, swooping out over the city, occasionally crashing into plate glass windows. When bored or frustrated, the men quit their jobs without notice, and stay at home to watch soap operas and preen in front of bathroom mirrors. Even the best working men quit their jobs as soon as they have children of their own. For who better to raise the children than their own fathers? Who better to love them, tend to their every need, and teach them how to follow in the footsteps of their fathers and mothers in accordance with the Island tradition? Who better to support their wives' careers? As it is often said on the Island: beneath every great Island woman there is an angelic Island man.

On the Island where I come from

parents worship their daughters. They invest all their hopes for the future in their girls, spoiling them rotten, letting them do and have whatever they wish. When I was a boy, my family was no different. While my sisters were allowed to go out night after night, I was never out of my parents' sight. Like all proper Island boys, I knew I had to remain a virgin. I had to keep my reputation as clean as freshly bleached linen. But by the time I was twelve, I wanted to go out on the town. I wanted to fly around after dark. *It's not fair*, I complained. *My sisters don't have to abide by the rules. Why do I?* My father said what he always said. *You aren't a girl, son. God didn't make us equals.*

Until I was eighteen, my father kept me indoors, checking on me after he turned out the lights. A homemaker and charm-school graduate himself, he was forever tidying the kitchen and garden as well as my hair, my wardrobe and my changing moods. He knew when the first sign of desire crossed my mind, and when I kissed my neighbor, Angelina, on the sly. He knew when I smoked my first cigarette and drank beer with the cool kids after school. And he knew when anger flared beneath my obedient smile. *Anger*, he said, *is unbecoming of a proper Island boy.*

On the Island where I grew up

my sisters were natural performers, singers, ballerinas, and lovers of men. Food was their code for some kind of romantic act, and sometimes for a specific guy. A flirtation was a fizzy drink like an Orange Crush or a Pepsi. Diet Coke meant something exciting might happen soon. Pretzels and chips were holding hands. Kissing, mango flan. But one year, they all liked the same man. Payday, they called him, after the imported candy bar with peanuts and chewy caramel, a candy we could never get enough of back then. I think of him sometimes even now, his brown curls and freckles, his sneering grin. How he blushed when my sisters teased him, how they kept spinning around and around him, stealing his wallet, his books, his cigarette lighter from the back pocket of his jeans, dipping his waistband to show off his tattoo of a flowering plant. I remember the last night my sisters danced, all on a single stage in a park with a beautiful arboretum, and how Payday clapped and clapped. That was the night my sisters looped their arms through his, took him away, and did not come back in for some time. The night I felt their music rise like a moon tide, their laughter and song lifting higher and higher, as if it would never subside. I rarely saw Payday after that night, though I glimpsed him once or twice on the streets, his head hung low, his shirt untucked. He always turned away. He looked oddly adrift to me then, like a candy wrapper tossed by a gust of wind.

On the Island where I come from

the law holds men responsible for all unwanted pregnancies. A man who denies paternity of his own son will be exiled. A man who denies paternity of his daughter can have his balls removed. As a result many men are unhappy with what they call *the women's laws*. They talk nostalgically of the good old days when men covered their bodies in cloaks with hoods, and never once looked a woman in the eye before marriage. Back then there was no such thing as a girl taking a guy for a test-drive. There was no kicking the tires, no testing the wipers or lights. In those days a man was considered good enough just because he was alive. Because he was—at least as soon as he had a daughter and a wife. Back then people respected the wishes and commands of the divine.

The House Husbands

Most Islanders consider childcare the man's job. Men are responsible for raising well-mannered children. *If you're going to hang around the house all day*, an Island woman will tell her spouse, *then you can at least take better care of the children.*

The men complain that they are no longer allowed to use the old techniques (the tried and true) for disciplining the young. They long for the good old days when fathers used sleeping potions to quiet their screaming offspring for a few delicious hours every afternoon. From 3:00 to 5:00 PM the fathers regained their peace of mind, watched TV, swung on porch swings, and talked with the neighbors. When the children woke, everyone was in a better mood.

It seemed so harmless, the fathers contend, those little white masks, doused in chloroform, pressed briefly over a child's nose and mouth, and the immaculate silence that followed. What harm could that have caused? Especially on those endless summer days when the children wake with the sunrise, and the cocktail hour threatens never to arrive.

On the Island where I grew up

for Emily Lisker

no one believed me when I told them I grew up in a family of magicians. They didn't believe that my mother knew how to appear and disappear at will. To the locals she was simply a master chef, baker, and the owner of a popular kiosk in the center of town. They didn't know that when she baked pastries and cakes, she stirred in her memories of bliss and last night's dreams. Or that she could bend men and children and clouds into any shape she wished. Like all magicians, my mother wanted an apprentice, but she didn't know which of her children had inherited the gift.

So she made us take lessons. The first lesson she taught us was how to cut each other in half. Then in quarters. We practiced late into the night, competing to see who was best with invisible knives. Many nights we stayed up late and danced without our heads. We played music without our thoughts, our lips, our breath. Even the dogs joined in. So my mother cut off their heads, too. Without their heads, the dogs couldn't bark at the moon. They couldn't wake the neighbors. My sisters and I and the dogs could dance to our hearts' content without anyone saying she was too tired or hungry or nuts. Without anyone hearing a single shout or whine or fight. In this way we were always good friends and neighbors and citizens, and we became accustomed to living in smaller and smaller parts. No one, not even our mother, with all her magic, could stitch us together again.

On the Island where I grew up

after the lights were turned out, I watched the shadows glide across the ceiling and walls and take on the forms of the dead as I fingered the tag on my blanket and pulled buttons off my nightshirt. *What if ghosts are real?* I whispered, trying to see if my sisters were awake. *What if God makes mistakes? What if there are too many mean, bad folks on the earth? And ugly ones, too, and ones who look half-baked?*

Shut up! my sisters shouted, sitting up in their beds, their faces framed by moonlight. *Shut up right now!* And I did. That's when I loved my sisters best. When they made the darkness still, when they silenced my night terrors, and I could sleep at last.

Years later, when I left my childhood home, I was all alone with my fears. I didn't sleep a wink. I haven't slept through a night since.

On the Island where I come from

the cooks were the most revered members of society, admired alongside the painters, the sculptors, the dancers, and the architect of the governor's mansion. That's why my mother, a chef in her own right, was so well known. My mother baked a special pastry that she sold from a kiosk on the plaza in the middle of town. In the mornings she woke before dawn and rolled out the dough made from rice flour, almond oil, and salt. She filled it with a paste of honey, nutmeg, and mamees—an orange tropical fruit that tastes of apricots and summer rain. Sometimes, if the mood struck her, she would add a little something else. It was that something else everyone loved. No one knew what it was or why. (Only I, her son, was allowed to spy on her and see what it was, but to this day, I haven't told a soul.) My mother always said that everyone has an essence without a name that is her special additive, her gift to life, love, pastries, and soup.

But there were rumors that her pastries were enchanted. For certain men, the pastries inspired such desire that with each bite, they felt greater and greater hunger. Before the men could stop themselves, they would begin to weep. *More! Please! More!* Islanders would hear their wails all through the town. The men had to be stopped from competing with the pigeons that pecked at the crumbs on the city streets. Some were taken away by police. Others accused my mother of crimes, insisting she was a witch or a part of the female conspiracy whose sole purpose was to keep the Island men hungry, desperate, enslaved.

But my mother blamed the men. She said men are born with so much greed, they can never be satisfied. Back then she was too busy to notice me, a small boy, crawling beneath her counter, licking the crumbs from the floor and my sticky fingers and knees. If I didn't lick quickly, tiny red ants would race up my body, biting into my sticky skin, mistaking me for a tropical fruit.

On the Island where I come from

bakers and chefs are featured in newspapers and slick magazines alongside articles about the president, the economy, tidal waves, and recent insect infestations. Every so often a gossip columnist claims to reveal a secret recipe from a renowned chef, and scandals and lawsuits erupt. Only on rare occasions are the recipes authentic, but everyone tries them just the same. *100 Recipes for Mango Cream Pie* is a feature every summer in *Gala*, the Island's best-selling magazine, along with *The 99 Secrets to Hot Sex You Never Knew*. The ingredients of the pies, like the recipes for sex, have everything to do with the fruit, when it was picked, whether it was green or overripe, how long it was left on the shelf, and if it was handled with love or anger or regret. A good cook knows the perfect balance between sweetness and relief. Too much of a good thing, one falls asleep. Too little, one feels a tinge of regret.

On the Island where I come from

the women are sexual aficionadas like women nowhere else on earth. The women can make love until every pore on their bodies opens and sends bliss into the horizon like an Island sunrise, reflecting the sky, the sea, the earth. Their lovemaking can last for eight days and eight nights. The women are acrobats in the sack. But Island men like men everywhere, lack patience and often rush for an imaginary finish line. Many Island women prefer to make love to women rather than bother with the men who simply soil their sheets. But it is not unusual for an Island woman to keep a male harem on the side. She reasons that if it takes eight men to satisfy her, why not keep nine? Of course other women claim that men should be trained like circus animals to perform in the bedroom and beyond. That's why the Island's man-trainers can be seen riding their men down city streets time and again. Some keep their men on leashes. Others prefer halters or diamond-studded bridles, but whips and spurs are never used. The men, it is said, will do anything to please if you give them the right treats. A good meal often works just fine. But most will do a lot for a bit of praise, and anything for a round of thunderous applause.

On the Island where I come from

all the women look like Angelina Jolie. The women like to call themselves Angelina, even if their real names are Rose, Pilar, Isabella, or Felicia. Many claim that Angelina Jolie is from our Island, but she doesn't know this because her parents stole her away when she was an infant. The women love to talk about their relationship to Angelina. They say that Angelina is their cousin, their niece, their long-lost child. Like Angelina, they all have hair the color of crow's wings, and lips fat from centuries of sucking mollusks from the sand. The women are proud of their heritage and say they are the last humans to emerge from the sea. Their hair smells of seaweed, their skin of low tide. Occasionally one of our women is born with webbed hands and feet. Like Angelina, our women are fertile. So fertile that a single woman can populate an entire town. Some, according to legend, have populated entire nations. Even if they can have no children of their own, the women adopt them. They adopt lost souls, too: street children, dogs, cats, pigeons, dolphins, angry men, and the sharks who swim close to taste the blood when it flows freely from between their swimming legs, but who rarely bite our women. Yes, even the sharks are loved by our women. The women know, as only women can, the difference between sharks who open their mouths wide to say *I love you, Angelina,* and sharks who are too hungry to know the difference between dinner and love.

On the Island where I grew up

the women sat on their porches at dusk, enjoying the Island breeze and watching the men walk past, admiring their hair, their legs, their style. Back then stretchy pants were all the rage. Some of the men wore tight pants; some wore tighter pants, and some men wore pants so tight, the women wondered if they could breathe. The women, including my mother and sisters, hooted and shouted when a sexy man walked past. *Did you see that guy?* one might ask. *I'd like to pinch his ass.* Sometimes, when they saw a particularly beautiful buttocks or set of thighs, they clapped and broke into applause.

It's so humiliating, I told my father. Even my neighbor, Angelina, liked to whistle when an attractive man walked by.

Girls will be girls, my father sighed. *Just like God will be God,* meaning that nothing I did or said could ever change these facts.

On the Island where I come from

the men are so beautiful, scientists fly in from distant countries to study the genetics of Island beauty. Research on the men has determined that male beauty is linked to laziness. Lying in hammocks all day, the most beautiful of our men don't even bother to get up for days at a time. The wealthiest Island women keep them in style and allow them to languish in luxury, lying back on silk sheets in air-conditioned bedrooms where they daydream or gaze longingly at their reflections in the mirrors that line their ceilings and walls. They love their reflections that much. They especially love to admire their curvaceous thighs. Such beautiful thighs our men have. As Julio Vega, our Island beauty king said in his famous ad for coconut oil, filmed on a beach with women massaging his glowing quads, *How I pity men who lack legs such as mine.* Islanders often repeat that line, and then they stroke their thighs and laugh and sigh.

On the Island where I come from

the men are written up in tourist magazines that describe them as Island Adonises. Even foreigners who consider themselves immune to desire cannot look upon the Island men without feeling a pang in the back of their throats and deep in their groins. But beauty has its price tag. Island men are often stalked, harassed, and picked up by strangers in dark vans, never to be seen again. Rumors spread of Island men being sold, shipped to foreign cities, and kept nude in cages where they can be admired and enjoyed at street carnivals in Europe and beyond. As a consequence the men are terrified. They develop nervous tics, tapping their fingers on tables, looking over their shoulders, smoking fragrant cigarillos, lighting one from the embers of the other. They fear solitude, dark alleys, and footsteps that chase them, even in dreams, through unlit streets. The sound of a car door opening in an empty parking lot can send them sprinting aimlessly for hours on end. Some grow so afraid, they fly away, lifting up into the air and just out of reach of grasping hands as wings unfold from their shoulder blades like sails. It is true, the stories that our men are the last living descendants of the angels. Alas, even their wings cannot save them. Foreigners with huge nets capture them as if they were giant butterflies. It is said on our Island that beauty is only the beginning of terror. And every angel is terrified.

On the Island where I come from

there are many stories about why the Island men grow wings. In one story, the Island men are said to be the last living descendants of the angels. Blown from heaven in a moment of God's wrath, the winged men landed on the Island where they were rescued and nursed back to health by Island women. For this reason, they are forever in the Island women's debt. They serve the women however they can, cooking their meals, cleaning their homes, and raising their children. In another story the Island men are considered an endemic species, much like Darwin's finches. The wings, it is speculated, once helped the Island men escape from predators. Why only the men have wings, no one knows.

But in the most popular story, wings evolved as a way for Island men to attract mates. After all, the Island women prefer men with wings. Wings are considered the essence of the Island male's mystique, much as blond hair or large breasts are a part of the feminine mystique in Europe and America. For all Islanders know that men with big wings are the most desirable. And foreign men are as appealing as eunuchs. The wings are what set the Island man apart. Wings are that something extra all Island women seek. Food and sex and money are never enough for her. She wants more, always more. An Island woman wants to fly. And not just in her dreams.

On the Island where I come from

casinos are especially popular among tourists. Most popular are the lotteries in which the winning men (or the partners of the winning women) have the honor of being paraded through the streets with our Island beauty kings, dressed in our native clothing: clingy pants and filmy shirts, left unbuttoned to allow passersby a glimpse of their chest and abdominal muscles and the colorful Island tattoos of flowering vines that begin at the navel and extend below the belt, ringing the phallus with native blossoms. Of course most foreigners refuse to tattoo their genitals in the manner of real Islanders and choose instead a temporary, washable design, painted on with feather brushes. But one foreign journalist wrote of the unbearable pain he endured while acquiring a penile tattoo. For weeks after he had nightmares that a large bird was pecking his penis.

On the Island where I come from

no woman will make love to a man who keeps his genitals *au naturel*. Instead the Island women admire the men with ornately tattooed penises. The more genital tattoos a man has, the more desirable he is. Island boys, as young as five or six, are ashamed of their undecorated penises and can't wait for the day when they, too, will possess penises as lovely as their dads'. Of course, foreigners consider phallic decoration to be a form of genital mutilation. Imagine, they say, burning the shapes of flowers and leaves into the tender pink skin. The pain of the tattoos is said to endure for weeks and sometimes months with possible side effects including diminished sexual appetite, delayed orgasms, infection, and on rare occasions, death. But beauty, Islanders claim, has its own logic. And sustained sexual bliss is best attained with a beautiful penis.

On the Island where I come from

it is said that God, Herself, pines for the Island man as She looks down at him from the heavens. *If only*, She thinks. If only She could hold him as She did once upon a time in the days before the Island man fell from Her grace. Her longing, She knows, is the only gift She can give him. On summer days the air glows with Her desire. Sometimes the Island man can barely open his eyes without going blind. He, for his part, dreams of Her, too. Sometimes he has visions from which he never recovers. He walks naked out into the town and then ascends, flying heavenward as fast as he can, never to be seen again. God feels sorry for him then, but there is nothing She can do to stop him from trying to reach Her. She knows the only thing worse than desire is not death. It is the end of desire.

On the Island where I come from

vagina envy is the most common psychological disorder. Island therapists do their best to cure it, but to no avail.

Behind the beard, the beers, the machismo, and the biceps, there lurks many a man who suffers from vagina envy. Those afflicted feel as lost as a rowboat adrift at sea.

No one knows the cause of the sickness, though Island psychologists blame the early weaning of male children. A boy should be suckled until he is three years old. Otherwise he grows up with an insatiable hunger for a woman's breast and is doomed to a life of unbearable rage and lust.

In cultures where the sickness is rampant, women are despised for their laughter, their wisdom, and their sexuality. The hatred becomes a fire that spreads from man to man. Untreated, the hatred grows until it cannot be contained. Men become so overwhelmed with vagina envy, they dream of burning women and girls at the stake or stoning them in the plaza at the center of town.

Some of the symptoms of the disease are subtle. A young man in one study refused to go out at night. He became moody, distant, and rarely saw friends. Alone, he stared at the wall, and when asked if he was okay, he didn't answer. He couldn't. He was drowning in a sorrow so deep, the words would not rise from his throat.

Like most men who suffer from vagina envy, he blamed a woman for all that hurt inside him, for all the emotions he could not explain, and for his feeling of irreparable loss.

There is no known cure for vagina envy, though the women on the Island assure men that if they lead a good and honest life, they will be reborn as women in the next life.

On the Island where I come from

many Island men and boys suffer from sleepless nights, especially in the poorest neighborhoods. They often wake to lights flashing, doors slamming, and people shouting. Everyone knows what this means. Boys are being taken from their homes. They are sold in the wee hours of the morning.

Sometimes a fight breaks out. A father tries to hold on to his son. A boy runs away. The police get involved. The trafficking of young boys is illegal of course, but the police are easily bought. Pretty boys can bring a high price. A black market thrives.

And what better way to protect the young boys, some Islanders argue, than to sell them to wealthy women where they will be trained in the art of pleasing. At least then they will not be preyed upon by foreigners and sold like exotic pets.

The local name, the gross idiom, for pretty boys is green sugar. Island boys are said to be as sweet as the unbleached sugarcane children suck, the juice running down their chins and staining their cotton shirts.

Miles from the inner city, in the gated communities of the wealthy, the Island matriarchs teach their newly purchased boys how to clean, babysit, and tend the vegetables and chickens. Only after the boys reach puberty does their real work begin.

On the Island where I come from

a hardworking woman is most admired. A hardworking woman is an Island archetype. It is said that a hardworking woman is both master and slave, boss and lackey, hunter and hunted, goddess and lady. My mother tried her best to become a hardworking woman. But like most magicians and chefs, she was too dreamy, too easily lost in thought. In the middle of a day or sentence, she would forget where she was and suddenly stop and gaze at an eagle flying overhead, a surfer riding a distant wave, or a black cat walking on the beach. Nevertheless, she tried her best.

Let's go! she cried every day before dawn as she rushed out of bed, barely pausing to brush her teeth. *Let's slay some wild beasts.* No matter how fast she ran, no matter how many tasks she completed, it was never enough. From time to time, she whipped herself to make herself work a little harder. She whipped and whipped herself. She didn't want to grow soft.

At the end of each day, she thought of all she didn't accomplish. She made a long list of things she failed to do and read it over and over—her evening litany of failures. Soon she was inconsolable and began to sob. *Tomorrow,* we would tell her. *Tomorrow is another day. You will feel better tomorrow.* And when tomorrow came, she did feel better. She rushed out of bed before the sun rose, coffee cup and whip sack in hand, shouting, *Carpe diem, carpe diem,* the day fleeing like a phantom before her.

On the Island where I come from

the hardworking woman is forever in search of the ideal whip. She never wants to slack off on the job, so she needs the perfect whip to whip herself into shape. The perfect whip changes with her age and the season and the latest styles. The selection at the Island whip shop is always overwhelming. As the sales clerk explains, there are all kinds of whips for all kinds of women. There are whips for the nubile, whips for the newlyweds, whips for the crones, whips for the professionals, whips for the whip-masters, whips for the first-time whippers. There are whips of nylon, whips of kangaroo-hide, whips of snakeskin, whips of silk, and whips of cotton and other natural fibers. There are whips that are for delicate moments, whips that leave lasting impressions, whips that barely whip but are mere suggestions of a whip. And for the collectors of whips there are designer whips and whip accessories including whip holsters, whip tote bags, whip badges and lockboxes in case one must leave her whips at home when on vacation. Every hardworking woman knows her whip is for herself alone. Her whip is the meaning of her life. The hardworking woman never shares her whips with anyone else, not even her lover or spouse. Every man knows that he must discover what really whips his woman if he wants to possess her. For to know a woman's whip is to know the secret she would never tell a soul, not even herself.

On the Island where I come from

only women hold political office. During every election season at least one angry man runs for mayor, governor, or even president. The angry man tries to rally others to his cause of male liberation. He flaps his wings wildly, thrusts his fist in the air, and shouts demands for equal rights, pay, respect, and representation. Of course, nothing happens. Everyone knows nothing will change on the Island. Nevertheless, the women are concerned. They know men are unstable. Men are like paper. They catch fire easily, and the fire can spread. For this reason the women do their best to calm the angry man. They bring him to Dolly, the Island's most accomplished man-trainer who wraps him in warm towels and touches him with soothing oiled hands. She listens until he is quiet at last. Then she stretches him back in her hammock and teaches him how to feel the wind drop or rise or change directions on the hairs of his head until he can tell if there will be fair skies or storms in the next hour, day, or week. There is always a need for a human barometer, Dolly tells him, but there is never a need for troubling thoughts and sleepless nights. She keeps the angry man until he rests peacefully, his head on her breast. Until he wakes in the morning unable to remember who or what he is. *Dolly?* he asks. He is happy just to hear her say *yes*.

On the Island where I come from

Dolly Delita is a world-famous man-trainer. Author of the best-selling *Obedience Training for Men at Home and in the Workplace*, Dolly has spent her life working with all kinds of men. Given the right circumstances and incentives, a man can become as useful as a woman, she claims. Despite his undesirable proclivities, a man can transform into an intelligent, obedient, and adoring human being.

The current consensus on the Island is that men must be treated with a firm and experienced hand. Men must learn who is alpha, who is really in command. Gone are the sixties when everyone was out in the streets, preaching love and peace and equality. Our new Island president, in her inaugural address, blamed men for the current shortage of tortillas, beer, marijuana, and mulberries, as well as the steep increase in crime. All the wars that have ever happened, she said, are evidence of what beasts men are when in command. The right-wing pundits say the demise of the world is caused by men.

Dolly Delita disputes these claims. In a filmed interview, she talks casually before the cameras and exhibits an array of counterexamples. Her middle-aged man, José, who was once a beauty king and ran for president, rests his head on her lap and eats plum after plum from her hands. Max and Lorca, her brazen teenagers, former delinquents who refused to remain virgins, are happily weeding her garden and tending her pigs and goats. And Alfonso, her oldest man, works in the kitchen, skinning potatoes. He was once tossed out on the streets by his Angelina, and Islanders thought he would never stop howling at the moon. He's old and grizzled around the chin, and his mind is going dim. But she would never throw him out and replace him with a younger man. Nor would she put him in a special home as Island women do with their older men. He's her soulmate, she explains. He's her oldest and best friend.

On the Island where I come from

St. Julio's Finishing School is the Island's elite academy for boys. Any boy who wishes to attend St. Julio's must have his blood tested to determine whether he possesses the right genetic material to attend such an exclusive institution.

St. Julio's boys are destined to become true paragons of their gender, capable of mastering the fine art of marital bliss. St. Julio's promise, complete with a money-back guarantee: all its graduates marry once and forever.

As part of their education, the boys who attend St. Julio's participate in seven wedding ceremonies per week. The back rooms and wings of the school serve as sanctuaries where simultaneous weddings take place every day except Monday, a day designated for sanitation and janitorial training. All St. Julio's graduates are trained as chefs, servers, babysitters, dishwashers, and janitors in addition to their marital lessons.

Each student develops a special ceremonial skill. Those who are good with their hands become either calligraphers who compose hand-lettered wedding invitations, or seamsters who design and mend bridal gowns and suits. These boys are often seen attending to last-minute clothing emergencies for members of the weddings.

Other boys with an artistic flare learn to arrange flowers, hair, and makeup and are expected to apply the finishing touches to bridal parties, dabbing cheeks with color, pinning long tresses into the traditional Island up-dos, sometimes adding pearled barrettes or glittering brooches shaped like tropical fruit or birds.

Musical students sing or play the organ or the flute while the cake is being cut and the champagne is served.

All students take turns filling the pews of sparsely attended weddings, a practice they continue long after leaving the academy. It is believed on the Island that the more witnesses at a wedding ceremony, the stronger the couple's vows. And the stronger the marriages, the happier the future is for all Islanders. Wedded bliss is considered the highest spiritual status an Island man can attain.

The graduates of St. Julio's Finishing School for Boys learn to love weddings so much that when they fall asleep at night, they dream of the day when they, too, will walk down the aisle. Asleep or awake, they cry whenever they watch the groom kiss the bride. They know that this kiss is the pinnacle of every man's existence, and everything that follows is but a shadow or afterthought, and the beginning of his inevitable demise.

On the Island where I come from

Relinquishing Self was a standard lesson taught in Island schools for boys, and could be found in the opening chapter of *An Island Boy's Guide to Life*, a classic Island text. In "Relinquishing Self," Island boys were taught to visualize their ambitions, desires, and dreams for personal glory and self-aggrandizement, then asked to contemplate how selfish their dreams were. For one boy to win, they learned, another must lose. For one boy to become rich, another must become poor. For one boy to be happy, another must be sad. *You don't want to bring sorrow into the world, now do you?* the teacher would ask. She taught them about the American and European cultures where individual and personal greed are glorified, and wars, environmental destruction, and sexual abuse are the natural consequence. *A country that celebrates greed is a country that celebrates death*, the teacher proclaimed, *not only of people and faith and ethics, but also of our world's oceans, forests, and animals.* The boys shuddered. How can men be so evil? they wondered. They were then taught how they could grow up to be good and compassionate men who would willingly sacrifice their own wishes for power and glory so that others, especially the Island women and children, might be served rather than oppressed. In this way, the teacher said, all Islanders will live happily and peacefully ever after.

On the Island where I come from

the most popular toy for boys is the charming Boberto doll, notable for its exaggerated male attributes, luxurious black hair, and mysterious smile. While some Islanders consider these dolls to be a sexist depiction of the male gender, the dolls remain a bestseller with the average Island boy owning at least seven Bobertos. Toy stores on the Island sell Bobertos for every occasion including the ever-popular Holiday Boberto, dressed in hunter green trousers and a crimson silk shirt, unbuttoned to the navel to reveal Boberto's Island tan and classic muscular silhouette, and the sizzling Summer Boberto, dressed in a sporty safari outfit and a matching sun hat. If you pull Summer Boberto's drawstring, he transforms into Swimmer Boberto in an azure Speedo and flippers. Summer Boberto's accessories include a swim mask, suntan oil, and a diary with a golden key and the words *I love Angelina* inscribed in tiny letters on every page.

On the Island where I come from

both male and female children have mango-sized brains, but in adolescence the male brain expands, due to a sudden hormonal flood. The larger size is needed to accommodate the male's biological needs: the stretching of his bones, muscles, and wings. Everyone can see the transformation as it occurs. First the head begins to swell, then the feet and hands. Soon the arms hang long and limp by the boy's sides. He hunches his shoulders, looks down or away, as if he could hide his desperation, the sudden turmoil and aches and twinges, the pain like a thousand insects fluttering beneath his skin. He twitches all day and night and wishes he could curl back into the boy he was yesterday, last week, or last year. Soon enough, he knows, he will have to learn to fly. He will leap into the waiting air. His body will make sure of that, even as he cries out silently, *No, please, no!*

On the Island where I grew up

my favorite Boberto dolls slept on my pillow beside me at night, long after I was too old to play with them. My first Boberto was Student Boberto, a smiling Boberto dressed in an Island boy's school uniform: a plaid button-down shirt, black leather shoes with gold buckles, and tan, Lycra trousers. Student Boberto's accessories included black-rimmed glasses, a satchel with a miniature textbook, *An Island Boy's Guide to Life*, and a lunch box filled with tiny snacks. But the Boberto I loved most was Teenage Boberto with his soft flowing curls, silk floral blouse, and crimson wings. Teenage Boberto's accessories included a gold bowtie, a tuxedo, and a velvet box containing a sparkling engagement ring. If I pressed his bellybutton, Teenage Boberto would sing, *Come fly with me, let's fly, let's fly away*, as his wings opened and closed like clapping hands.

On the Island where I grew up

when I was a boy, I confided in Angelina, the girl next door. I told her all my dreams: how I wanted to be an engineer or an architect. I wanted to design houses, ships, airplanes, and rockets. I complained that there were no science or math teachers at St. Julio's School for Boys. I had no male role models or education in these areas. When I complained at school, my teachers suggested I give up my ambitions. *Only women have careers*, they said.

It's so unfair, Angelina agreed. *You should be able to study whatever you want. Why can't you become an architect?* A true idealist, she said that when she grew up, she'd start a coeducational school where boys and girls were treated equally. Where sexism was not allowed. Tossing back her long, black hair, sucking on a cigarette, she added that even the size of my wings (or lack thereof) didn't matter to her. Of course, that was before she met a man with extra-large wings and never looked at me again.

On the Island where I come from

the most popular books among school boys were the Super Girl books starring girls who saved the world from imminent destruction. Also popular were the Island myths about girls who could breathe underwater, see the future in a mirror, and escape their own shadows. Back then Islanders believed in the power of feminine magic. Everyone knew, for example, that Island girls could speak to the birds and collect them like seashells from the sky, keeping the pretty ones in cages, much as Island women kept their men.

Sometimes, after school, I watched my neighbor, Angelina, climb the ceiba tree outside my window. Still dressed in school clothes, she shinnied up the trunk, climbed out on a branch, and waited for the birds to fly into her open hands. How I envied her then, and how I envied the birds she stroked so tenderly, envy like a stone lodged in my young boy's heart.

On the Island where I come from

a man is defined by his wingspan. The bigger the wingspan, the more desirable the man. But some Island men's wings remain embarrassingly small. These men can seek medical help, but wing enhancement is a costly process, achieved by regular injections of a neurotoxin found in the venom of thups, a tiny crimson insect indigenous to the Island. The venom, it is said, interacts with the male hormones, causing the body to act as if it were a teenager, still sprouting wings, pimples, and pubic hairs. Side effects include depression, nausea, night sweats, and, in extreme cases, halos. Thup-therapy, as it is known, must be continued throughout a man's lifetime. Otherwise the man will lose his wings, slowly at first, a feather at a time—then more rapidly, the feathers falling like petals on the street behind him. Islanders giggle at a man who is losing his feathers. *He looks like a plucked chicken!* they say as he walks past. When his last feather falls, the man will leave the Island in shame. Neither he nor his wings will ever return.

On the Island where I grew up

I still remember my first flying class. How the instructor called out, *This is how it's done!* as he leapt into the air, his arms flung outwards as he ascended. Spreading his wings wide, he flapped slowly and gracefully as he glided around the classroom, his shoes just skimming the hair of the tallest boys. We students stared open-mouthed, our wings fluttering from our backs in nervous anticipation. But when we tried, we were out of control, crashing into light fixtures and ceiling fans before plummeting to the floor in a shower of feathers. Even the most graceful boys swooped at odd angles before skidding to the floor in lopsided landings. There were so many bruised elbows and knees. The boys who learned the fastest were the same boys who grew too cocky and soared out of classrooms and over the Island, only to be found hours later, hanging from telephone wires or passed out beneath plate-glass windows, their eyes staring blankly at the sun. A few died in this way. Others were kidnapped by strangers. Still others were blown out to sea by the strong trade winds. Islanders watched them go, dipping and rising like crazed butterflies, their bodies growing smaller and smaller until they were nothing but a shimmer on the horizon.

On the Island where I grew up

I tried to become the ideal boy: as sculpted and slender as a ballet dancer. Every morning when the sun rose, I worked out with barbells before the metal became too hot to grasp, and sweat ran in rivers and burned my eyes. Then I raced through the city streets and beaches, my feet just skimming the ground. I was careful not to lift off. But occasionally, in an unguarded moment, my wings opened, and I rose over the heads of pedestrians. Tourists watched open-mouthed as I ascended and descended quickly and went red with shame, hoping no one would catch me and give me a ticket. It was against the law to fly in the city. Some politicians wanted to ban flying everywhere. It was too dangerous, they said. Too many Island boys were kidnapped by foreigners the moment they landed. But I was desperate to be as slender as the models on the pages of slick magazines, and nothing burns calories or builds muscles quicker than flight. (It was also easy money, too. When I landed, strangers tucked envelopes of cash deep in my pants pockets, their fingers lingering as long as I allowed.) Afterwards I was always starving, but instead of food I sipped InstaCal, a pink powder mixed with water that replaced electrolytes and created a brief sensation of satiety. It was always a battle between the wish to be thin and beautiful but not as thin as the anorexic boys who lost their hair, their glow, their feathers. Chiseled and gaunt, I flexed my muscles in front of mirrors and shop windows, admiring my silhouette. Nights I dreamt I was flying away, my Angelina straddling me as she urged me upward. *Higher!* she gasped. *Higher! Higher!* as we rose together, riding the waves of the wind.

On the Island where I grew up

only men with hairless bodies are considered desirable to the opposite sex. As an adolescent, I was so afraid of my body's capacity to grow fur, I watched with horror as curly black hairs took over my back, my chest, my arms, and my legs, and created a small thicket above my penis. It was as if a shadow were taking over my body.

Sooner or later I knew I'd have to join the crowds of Island men who visited the local salons for monthly grooming sessions. The salons, the hubs of male social activity, were where my father and uncle caught up on the latest gossip and clothing styles. As a boy I watched them leave the house, hairy and grizzled, only to return hours later, as soft and smooth as nectarines.

Depilation

No one warned me how painful the process was. Or described how aestheticians in white robes and latex gloves would paint my skin from neck to toe in a viscous chemical paste before placing me under a heat lamp to dry. Men sat in plastic chairs and sipped wine or meditated as the paste hardened to a hot shell, slowly burning away the dead skin and lifting each hair from its follicle. As the master aesthetician explained, depilation is a spiritual practice, a preparation for sex and death. Visions of angels and gods were not uncommon at local salons.

I still remember my first time. When the pain became unbearable, a scream escaped my lips. I was surrounded by robed stylists who ordered me to hush as they poured shots of liquor down my throat, peeled me from my steaming shell, and led me to a bathtub filled with ice cubes. There I sat, shivering, drunk and alone, my burning skin as pink as a newborn's.

On the Island where I come from

the first signs of puberty happen at night. A boy wakes to feel a fire inside him, like an ache, a hunger, an indefinable wish, followed by the first prickling of wings. It hurts so much when the wings break through the flesh, each wing-bone a knife in the skin. (Picture it as the sharp beak of a baby bird pecking its shell. Only the shell is a skin full of nerve-endings.) Then there is the blood, the shame, the need to cover it up so no one will know. This, the boy learns, is how it feels to be a man. Nothing he does, says, or prays can ever make him feel safe from what he has become.

On the Island where I come from

pubescent boys wear absorbent pads on their backs when their wings are sprouting. The pads soak up the blood, though leakages occur, and boys often complain that they feel like the Hunchback of Notre Dame. By the age of sixteen most wings are fully formed. But in one out of ten cases, one or both wings stay lodged beneath the skin and must be surgically removed. Wing retention is usually caused by poverty or anorexia, for lack of nutrition inhibits proper wing development. Many boys envy their wingless friends who are not seen as sexual targets by the Island women or foreigners who compare our virgin boys to angels and will pay a high price to be the first to ride them.

On the Island where I grew up

I was only a boy when I first saw God. I remember the day exactly. I lived in a small neighborhood of white stone houses where all of the girls were called Angelina and all of the men were old. Every year tourists visited in the fall after the summer plague of insects had passed, when the air was reputed to be the purest on the planet. So pure was the air in fact, it appeared to contain tiny glass windows. Islanders liked to say that if you peered into these windows, you would see what heaven looked like. Gullible tourists spent their days staring at the shimmering air, seeking their own personal glimpses of eternity.

In those days the west side of the Island where I lived was new to foreigners. Few tourists ventured down our streets and beaches or visited our shops. We didn't yet know to mistrust them. So when a stranger took my hand and began stroking my arm and asked if I wanted to see God in all Her glory, I said yes. And when he began to undress me, explaining I must be naked first, I was merely surprised. But when he touched every part of my body as if it were holy, as if it deserved adoration, I thought he was making good sense. I had always secretly believed I should be worshiped, that I was an angel in disguise. God made a mistake by sending me to earth. When the sharp and sudden pain of penetration surged through me, I screamed and cried, and I don't know what happened after that. I must have passed out. When I woke, the stranger was gone. Blood was running down my thighs. But when I looked up, I did see God. God with the face of Angelina. And She held me in her soft, brown arms.

On the Island where I come from

everyone falls in love with Angelina. It happened to me when I was eighteen. We were walking on a white sandy beach at sunset, the wind just lifting her black hair, her red dress wrapping around her legs, and the sound of the waves and the gulls in our ears. We looked like an ad for eternal bliss. Strangers snapped our photographs, and Alpha World Airlines used the pictures in their brochures. *This is where Angelina vacations*, the ads read. What I remember best is how I sucked in and in for air. How something snapped inside me: a tiny bone in my heart, a splinter of pain I still feel. Staring out at the water, I watched a shimmer ripple across the surface, and tiny sails racing into the horizon. I try not to think now what I was thinking then.

After Angelina left me

my father comforted me as best he could. *You're better off without her*, he sighed, adding that he had never liked her. She was the wrong kind of girl, always eying loose men, cat-calling, pressing dollar bills in their pants. *All she wanted was to get into your trousers*, he said. I wished she had. I wished I hadn't refused her advances, claiming I wasn't *that kind of man*. Just imagining a night in bed with her still makes me cry. And wish for extra-large wings. Or some kind of revenge. I was so desperate then, I sought medical attention, asking a doctor for injections I could barely afford. I told the doctor I wanted to win Angelina back. *Of course*, she agreed. *But you know there are risks.* I was too young to worry. Too stupid to think of anything besides Angelina's soft, wide lips.

After Angelina left me

I felt like an utter failure as a young man. Everything about me was wrong, my blemished skin, my close-set eyes, my extra-small wings. No matter how often I shaved, I always grew an afternoon shadow. No matter how hard I worked out, I always looked plump in my own eyes. No matter what I wore or said, I didn't feel or sound all right. I was so tired of trying to be a nice boy. Tired of keeping the trophy between my legs untouched. All I really wanted was to be the kind of guy my father called *bad news* or *damaged goods*.

Loss

The year my wings no longer folded neatly across my back, everything fell away from me: my family, my feathers, my dreams. I had no money, no love, no life. I sat alone, watching the world through slats in my blinds. How I envied the other boys, the naïve young men who fluttered down the streets and hovered around shops and bars. They were the men Angelina trained, feeding them sugar cubes on her outstretched hands. She taught them how to sing and dance and fly on cue. What I would have done for a second chance.

But I grew old and featherless while they remained young, their skin professionally smooth, their wings luxurious and full, their hair and brows dyed a coppery brown—the favorite hair color back then was Julio Vega's *Sun Kissed*. I tried it, but my hair turned into an orange halo. And my eyebrows fell out. There wasn't a thing I could do right. My wings no longer folded neatly across my back. I had to give up, even though I knew to lose one's beauty is to lose one's manhood. All Islanders know that.

On the Island where I grew up

the past became a shadowy man I carried on my back, a twin whose eyes I was ashamed to meet. *Out of my bed!* I wanted to scream at the phantom that slept in my sheets. *Out of my mirror!* I wanted to shout when I flicked on the bathroom light. Each morning I shaved my chin and legs and above my lips. I plucked my eyebrows and covered my blemishes, dabbing them with cotton balls soaked in alcohol and special tinted creams labeled *wet sand* to match my summer skin and *almond bisque* for my wintry complexion. My trash basket overflowed with the fluffy white balls. But nothing I did could make me feel clean and new again. There was no washing away my sadness, no covering it with ointments or creams. No returning to the young man I once was, running down the sidewalks, glancing back to be certain no one was following me. *Little birds*, the women called us then. They watched us like sleepy cats from behind sunlit windows and doors.

A Bad Egg

You shouldn't be so sad, everyone said to me the year before I left. *You should learn to relax.* Their advice made me worry. The more I worried, the more miserable I became. Highly contagious, my misery spread like bad news. Men nodded and agreed when I complained about my life as an Island man. Women began whispering behind my back, *He's a bad egg.* My father and mother suggested a therapist.

Your case is untreatable, the therapist said.

I knew she was right. I wept every night. And during the days, my feathers came loose from my back, falling like shriveled leaves. No one noticed them. I was careful to keep my shirt tucked in, and wear a trench coat to hide my diminishing size. Thin and featherless, I looked like a walking coatrack.

While all around me Island friends were falling in love, marrying, fathering children, I lived alone. While they were proposing toasts to their newfound bliss, I had nothing to celebrate. I pretended indifference and even said I'd be happy to board the first ship to a distant land. Of course I had no choice. My flying days were at an end.

But for years after I left, I grew even more depressed. I felt a pressure in my chest and in the back of my throat. Angelina wrote me letters, saying she was still my friend. She kept me abreast of daily events. In my fantasies she wanted me back, but I was too proud to say yes.

This is what happens to a man who wants a vagina all to himself, my therapist had warned me. *He lives in his fantasies.* She was right. I didn't want to admit it. All I ever wanted was a vagina to call my own. Is that so much to ask?

My Secret

I never kissed a woman after Angelina. I keep that as my darkest
secret. The one I don't tell a soul. The one I never admit. The kisses,
like schools of fish, swam upstream without me. And long ago. See
how my lips droop, and my hands? Even my fingers are limp. These
are the signs. Don't laugh. I tell this to you who compare a kiss to
a rose, a kiss to a diamond, a kiss to a boat. (Not to mention what
happens next.) I want to say, *Shhh. Have mercy on me.* For I have heard
these things all my life. I have heard that a single kiss can save souls,
change the tides, the weather, the time of day. Even the afterlife. I
have heard a kiss is like clean underwear, something that makes you
feel better above and below. My Aunt Angelina told me that years ago,
bless her soul. (She died when I was twelve.) I have heard a good kiss
is like a Laundromat for the mind. It cleanses your thoughts. But only
if the kiss is the right kind. Then why, I ask you, why have I been so
denied? Why can't I buy a ticket to a kiss? Why can't I lasso a kiss like
a calf at a rodeo? Why can't I train a kiss like a tiger to jump through
hoops? Why can't I fly a kiss like a kite on a windy night? This I have
asked myself too many times as I crossed my arms across my chest and
drifted off to sleep. And I am asking again as I walk off alone into the
summer night, leaving my past behind like a dusty tent. I who am so
alone now that only the fireflies light up my nights.

On the Island where I come from

sometimes an Angelina, or the memory of an Angelina, slides under a man's skin. Once there, he might try to exhale her like smoke, but she will glide back in with each new breath. The man will smell her on his sheets and clothes and in the evening air. Sometimes he will think she smells like the sea, other times like a smoke-filled bar where he met her once, her voice as husky as a blues singer's. The mere scent of her will drive the heat through his blood. First his fingertips will go hot, then his toes. Then it will wash over him in a hot wave. For a while he might think he's only imagining things. That all he needs is a good night's sleep, but Angelina will never let him rest. She will keep him awake, tossing and stirring his dreams. When he gives up, he won't even bother to put on a robe. He will walk outside in the buff, let the wind cool his arms and legs. He will wander nude through the streets, calling, *Angelina!* He will know she's listening. But she will never answer his calls.

My Angelina

It didn't matter that you never spoke to me before I left, that you never answered my calls or letters. I believed in you. How could I help myself? I imagined that one day you would look up and say, *I want you. I need you. Hold me.* That when the sun touched your face, when the wind lifted your hair, when a strap of your dress slid from your shoulder, when you lips parted in a smile, it was only for me. Even in sleep, I repeated your name, as if it were magic, as if it were a spell. As if you really cared. *Albert,* you answered in my dreams. *Albert. My Albert.* Funny how you always called me Albert when I am not Albert. I answered all the same.

On the Island where I grew up

the therapist said, *Stand in Angelina's shoes, those shiny red heels she always wears, and you'll get it. How it really is for her.* The world is her own personal shopping mall. She wants a man? He's hers. You can only imagine how hesitant that makes her feel. How she leans forward, examining every detail. *May I help you?* a man might ask. But no. Not yet. She's still looking. Lingering. Taking her own sweet time. That's part of the fun, yes? Part of the turn-on. Knowing that whatever she wants, she gets.

This one, she finally says, leaning in for a kiss. And he's lost forever.

On the Island where I come from

psychotherapy begins with the traditional psychogram that produces a digital image of a patient's soul. In healthy patients the image looks like an apartment building with a million glowing rooms, each a lit box connected by squiggly lines. Island therapists explain that every box and line represents one of the many apartments in the mind and the connections between them, which are staircases and elevators one must take from time to time. Usually a person resides in one apartment or another, depending on her job, spouse, or state of mind. There are different names for the apartments as well as varying interpretations of their contents. Folks usually assume that the apartments on the top floor with the expensive view belong to the higher self, the feminine soul, and the muse. Far below is the lower self, though it isn't as low as many think. Not as long as an inhabitant can peer into its windows and see a few folks or scenes she wishes to forget but never can. There are apartments for the past self below as well, and the future self who often passes her on the staircase but never says hello. The fantasy self and the dream self are always trying to pick the locks of every apartment. In the basement is the tragic self who is only in love with bad news. The therapist's goal is not to control the rooms a client enters, but rather to be sure she glides easily from floor to floor, that the doors swing open, that no calcification has occurred, locking her forever in a dream or a basement or a childhood classroom. Song and seduction are the favored therapeutic techniques for increasing inner-flow, as is the practice of introducing the child one was to the Madonna on the 21st floor.

On the Island where I come from

the meaning of meaning is never taken for granted. Neither is the logic of logic. Or the story of stories. With any story, Islanders say, there is what happened, what one says happened, and what one wishes or pretends happened. There is life, there is death, there is the afterlife, and there is one's idea of all three. There is the dinner, the dirty silverware and plates, the late night aperitif (presented like a petit four on a china plate) and the digesting of them all, not to mention the headache the morning after.

Which is the most important? you might ask. Islanders don't answer such questions. Every answer you give, they turn into another question. It is the questions they love, the questions they say that lead to a state of wonder. Not the solutions. Not the beliefs.

On the Island where I come from

the buying and selling of souls is a lucrative business. Once the average Island man reaches middle age, he longs for a new soul. But a new soul should not be taken lightly and should never be too cheap or too expensive, too plain or too ornate, too soft or too silky. A new soul is the magic carpet that can glide a man smoothly into the heavens, while the old soul is a wounded bird that falls from grace again and again and is doomed to walk on earth like every aging man. The saleswoman promises a new soul of renewed life as she bargains away a man's old soul. She knows that every man in his forties wants to be someone else. Every man tries to hide his true self in a journal, a photo, a secret drawer. The new soul, the saleswoman promises, will feel as lovely and vibrant as adolescent wings. But there is no money-back guarantee.

On the Island where I grew up

a second-hand shop is not a respectable place. I know. When I was an outcast, I worked for a few months at a second-hand shop. Every day men filled the floor with bulging sacks of used clothes. *Stop!* I often said. *You have to stop buying the latest styles.* The men laughed in my face. Have you *seen* the new styles? they asked. I was too depressed to care about the difference between one year or day or outfit and the next. But I knew what they meant. I knew that Island men don't see fabric or color or style. When the Island men look at clothes, they see not pants or shirts or jackets, but success, money, sex. They see women unfastening their blouses, a button at a time. They see the future, too, as a warm wind billowing beneath their unbuttoned shirts; the past they bag and deposit to sleep on dusty shelves. Only a poor Island man who is down on his luck will wear the clothes of another man's years. This is, according to Island logic, the sure sign of a lost soul, though some debate which came first, the loss of the soul or the wearing of another man's slacks.

On the Island where I grew up

I once saw Frank Sinatra sipping tea at a local café. He sat beneath a peach-colored umbrella, reading the news and staring off into the horizon. *It's rude to stare*, my mother said, but he was so much whiter than the rest of the Island residents, I couldn't take my eyes off of him. I think he was the first famous foreigner I saw, though many followed. Elvis was at the café a week later. And one day I spotted Nijinsky running down a beach, leaping and leaping, his arms outstretched like a bird. I could tell he was jealous of the ease with which the Island men lifted into the air.

The famous, I learned then, are often so anxious they can't really die. They come to our Island instead, mistaking the Islanders for angels, and the Island for heaven. They come wanting to escape their tortured minds and fans, the heat of so many eyes watching their every move and blink or thought.

It's a strange thing, my mother said, *that whatever one most wants in life will one day become his curse. The famous think they want applause, but all the famous have ever really wanted is what everyone wants*, my mother said, meaning to be mothered. To be fathered. To be held in the soft, bare arms of an Island woman. To be enfolded in the wings of an Island man.

That is all anyone yearns for. But no one yearns like the famous. And so the Islanders take the famous into their arms and give them everything they have lacked, everything they have never had. *Yes*, the famous say. *Yes*, to whatever the Islanders ask, and they drift away at last, a beatific smile on their lips.

On the Island where I come from

there is a door to the land of the dead. Death's door, according to legend, is an ordinary door, though its knob glows, and light leaks from its frame. The door looks as if it is about to blow open and can barely hold back whatever waits on the other side. Some claim they have heard dogs barking from beyond, while others hear music, and others, the drumming of heavy rain. Still others claim to have heard their lost loved ones calling their names.

While it was once common knowledge where the door resided, its precise location is now top secret. Too many Islanders were opening it on a whim. Most were children who turned its shining knob on a dare, imagining they could catch a glimpse of what was on the other side. Of course, they were always sucked through, the door slamming behind them. No one ever returned with news.

After too many had vanished, the Island's president took it upon herself to hide the door. But when her political enemies began to disappear, people whispered. Now Islanders fear that a president might abuse her knowledge. For this reason all Islanders who are eligible, vote at elections. The more serene and soft-spoken a candidate, the more apt she is to be elected. Only the meek have ruled the Island for the last hundred years.

On the Island where I come from

thups arrive every June, but no one knows the exact day they will come. On early June mornings the Islanders open their doors a crack and peer anxiously outside. Standing on their porches, they scan the horizon for signs of the shimmering red insects. They wave at neighbors and hurry down the streets, listening to the chatter about the imminent arrival of thups. The owners of the neighborhood cafés busy themselves by lugging their patio furniture inside, and people everywhere seal up windows and doors. Duct tape is always in short supply. The residents of the Island are never friendlier than they are during the days of anticipation when they gather together to sip cinnamon tea, smoke their fragrant panatelas, and tell of last year's infestation when everything was so coated with thups one Russian immigrant swore it looked as if the town was coated with bubbling borscht—every house, office building, sanctuary, and bronze statue was alive with the fluttering red bugs. People love to tell the old wives' tales: thups are divine messengers, blown from God's topiary garden every year when the winds shift. Some say thup-bites caused the first orgasms to arrive on earth, though only the young thups, the nymphs, actually bite. Every year virgins race nude through the streets on the day the thups blow in, shouting, *The thups are coming! The thups are coming!* Islanders gather behind windows to watch the virgins run, sip champagne, and tell their own personal thup-tales, feeling communally intimate as scarlet clouds of insects descend.

After the thups take over the towns, everyone huddles inside, traveling through the underground passageways that connect every house and building in the city. When the first month of staying indoors is past, the people become so desperate, the only light in their lives emanating from one another's souls, they welcome near-strangers into their living rooms. Men and women share thup-tales at all hours of the day and night. One man shows off his boxes of thup-carcasses left over from last year's infestations. Dead thups, he says, rained from his books, china, and linens, despite all his efforts at cleaning and scrubbing. Another man exhibits the thup-smears on his bedroom walls where he swatted thups in the middle of a fever dream in which he saved his daughter, bringing her back from behind death's door. He says he still feels the touch of her small, cold hand. Another man describes how once, when he turned on the shower, wet thups like a cloud of steam filled the room, biting him in the most delicate places, and ever since that occasion, he has been an athlete in bed. A woman says her baby was bitten by so many thups, her first word was not "Mama," but God's first name—of course, the woman pressed the child to her breast for fear of what might happen next. (Breast milk is one of the few natural antidotes to thup-bites.) Everyone shudders inwardly as they listen, not wanting to talk of the Islanders who sing like the angels or grow halos after being bitten. They lean closer to reveal their darkest secrets, enjoying the feeling of illicit intimacy as they cling to one another, casting aside reason and restraint as if these were wool sweaters on a hot summer night. *If only we could live like this forever*, some sigh. But when the thups finally leave, the people return to their natural state of indifference, wearing sunglasses and avoiding one another's glances as if they had never met, much less peered inside each other's souls.

The Woman with the Halo

Most people are afraid of the woman with the halo. *What if the halo had happened to me?* they ask themselves. Some look down or away, and others avoid her altogether. Still others never mention the haloed woman or admit she exists. The children are the cruelest. They call her names like Moon Lady and Bug Lamp. But the farmers consider her a savior and bring her offerings of tea and soup and pastries filled with fruits and nuts and blessings. If it weren't for the haloed lady, they claim, insect infestations would ruin the annual crops.

The haloed woman tries to explain to anyone who will listen how her halo occurred. How she was left outside on a night in June when the thups arrived and was bitten at least a thousand times. Though she cried for help, no one would save her. Now nothing can be done to relieve her suffering. There is no known cure for halos. Summer nights are the worst, she says. She glows strongest when the weather is warm, and the bugs swarm around her head in great clouds, hissing, sizzling, and popping to the ground.

Scientists and journalists pester her from time to time, pressing her with inquiries, hoping to identify the properties of halo-bearing. She tells them how the magnitude of the halo varies, but that even a small child could manage a halo—in other words, it's less dangerous than it looks. True, a halo is not without risks, but as long as the halo hovers close to her head, she represents only a minimal fire hazard.

The real difficulty, she adds, is being so indelibly visible. She wishes she could simply blend in and hide her light inside herself as others do, or keep it under the proverbial bowl, though that metaphor never really worked for her. Once her mother made her a sleeping bowl out of ovenproof ceramic rimmed with silicone handles for easy removal. But not long after receiving the gift, she rolled out of bed, shattering the bowl and setting the hem of the bedspread on fire as the halo burst free.

These days when she can't sleep, and she often can't (it's so hard to sleep with a light on like that), the haloed woman stands outside on the street, glowing like a human star. *Excuse me*, she says to anyone within earshot. *Would you like a light?* Rare passersby stop. They lean toward her halo with their unlit cigarettes and linger for a moment, puffing smoke in her face and shooting the breeze. These are the happiest moments of her life, the moments when she chats and feels okay being here on earth. That's when she imagines herself as soothingly forgettable as any stranger, insomniac, or secondary character in a novel who can vanish into the world as easily as a sugar cube in hot water.

On the Island where I come from

there is an ongoing debate among academics as to whether one should give birth in summer or winter. *The Island Lady's Almanac* is frequently consulted in order to help fertile women make the right decision, but every woman already has her opinion. Advocates of a summer birth argue it is best to be pregnant in the harsh winter months and bring a child into existence when the air is warm, and the parents are relaxed, their days full of sunlight, fresh papayas, mulberries, and fish. The babies will grow strong enough to be weaned before winter, the months of colds and flu and Island depressions that are as oppressive as the winter fog that sinks into the bones, a state no mother wants to endure, much less feed to her infant in her blue, wintry milk.

The advocates of a winter birth claim it is best to bring a baby into the world in winter when there are no bugs, especially the Island thups, the tiny beaked beetles with crimson wings whose venom can cause irreversible damage, turning perfectly normal babies into God's chosen ones. Bitten baby girls might grow halos instead of hair, and the boys can develop voices that never deepen but instead rise with age, as is the way with all those who are destined for the heavenly choir. Equally troubling are the children who never synchronize themselves with time as it flows on earth. Their internal clocks are forever too fast or too slow, and cannot be reset. Living either in the future or the past, the children are incapable of being here now, and grow up into adults who miss all the important occasions of their lives, though they can tell you about them before or after the fact as fortune tellers, poets, or historians, and are often posthumously loved.

On the Island where I come from

death did not always exist. Death came by boat to the Island with the foreigners. Which ones, no one is sure. They say that the Spanish came first, then the English, then the Dutch. They came to take our gold, our land, our souls. When they had stolen everything they could and grew homesick for their own lands, they left. We were never so happy as the day we watched the last of them go. But as the last ship was setting its heavy sails and heading across the bay, several of our native women waved their arms and ran across the water to ask a few last questions of their priest. The priest, standing on the prow of the ship, was so surprised to see the women running on bare feet across water, he waved his arm in the air in a sign of the cross. At once the women sank like stones. In this way, the first converts on our Island were made. Some of the people on shore who watched the women sink became converts as well. They, too, began to die. This is how death came to our Island. To this day there are those who believe in death, and those who live forever. It is often debated which is the better way.

On the Island where I come from

everyone knows the truth about death. They know that the dead don't just vanish. Instead they hang around for days, amazed by what has passed. *I'm still here*, one might say to herself after she breathes her last. She might think she's fine until she notices the living or hears them ask, *Is she dead yet? Yes*, they will whisper as they hover above her.

You can die again and again, Islanders claim. And there are all kinds of deaths for all kinds of people. Some die so slowly, they pass before they ever pass away. Others fly out of life like kamikaze pilots, landing on the other side. Not a trace of them left, not even a whiff or a backward glance. Others shimmer and glow like sunsets on a summer night, putting on a show so that everyone says *ohh* and *ahhh*. Still others never pass away.

Which kind are you? That is the question every mother asks before a toddler takes a first step. The answer is the key to the future. If you know your end, Islanders say, your entire life makes sense.

On the Island where I come from

according to the story of creation, God created everything and its opposite in a single week. Thus there was day and night, earth and sky, woman and man. While woman was light, always carrying a glow in her belly like a small sun, man was cold like the moon, his only light a dim reflection of her own. While woman was soft and smooth, man was leathery and numb. Woman often wondered, when stroking man's hard belly at night, trying to warm and tame him as she had tamed the other animals, if he had swallowed stones instead of apples or plums. After all, he was always so hungry, always seeking more food and love, snuffling around for crumbs she had left behind. While woman slept peacefully, man stayed awake at night, staring at the stars, asking why he should trust this life that came in such small increments of time, or washed over him like waves as illogical and lovely as woman's mind. *What am I doing here?* he asked God. And *Why am I so small compared to the sky, so hairless and weak compared to the rest of the animals, so mortal and lost compared to You?* Night after night man raged against God, until at last She grew tired of listening to him. And so God created orgasms. After every orgasm, man fell into a sleep, deeper than the sleep of stones. And God at last was able to gain some peace of mind. But that was when woman began to complain.

On the Island where I come from

a favorite legend is the tale of St. Angelina, our Island's founding mother. St. Angelina, it is said, was once the most desired sex slave in all of Egypt. She was so beautiful, her body was known as the Promised Land, her lips the holy chalice, her bush the burning bush. Kings came from the East, drawn by the bright star of her beauty. Pharaoh himself lavished gifts of gold, frankincense, and myrrh upon her. But Pharaoh was troubled by repeated nightmares in which seventy-seven horses, all fat and fine steeds, drowned in a foaming sea, a dream no one could interpret but St. Angelina, whose gift of prophecy was as renowned as her gift of seduction.

But St. Angelina was crafty and never revealed the true meaning of Pharaoh's dreams. Instead she waited until God called down to her, *Run! Run for your life! And take the women with you!* That was the night Angelina freed the slave ladies, and together they fled from Egypt, and eventually discovered the promised land, the Island that is sacred to women.

But what happened to Pharaoh? you might ask. (This is the part of the tale the Islanders love best.) They say that Pharaoh and his army of seventy-seven horses and seventy-seven chariots chased Angelina and the slave women to the shore of the Red Sea, where Angelina parted the waves with a single touch of her index finger. Then she looked back and waved. Pharaoh, seeing the beautiful Angelina, glistening with sweat, her bare breasts touched by the first rays of sunlight, turned instantly into a pillar of lust and melted into the sand. And so did all his men.

And this is when every Islander who hears the story claps and claps.

On the Island where I come from

everyone knows it was Adam who ate the apple in the Garden of Eden. The snake had nothing to do with it. Adam didn't even apologize. Instead he grabbed the apple as soon as he thought God wasn't looking and bit into it greedily, the juice running down his chin. *No! Adam, no!* Eve cried, but Adam just grinned and grinned. The sense of wonder he felt then. And pride. How could he explain it? The sweetness on his tongue. The taste of rain, of summer, of rebellion. And the days that followed when all he wanted was to argue with Eve, and to win. *Who needs heaven? Or God?* he asked, when there is so much on earth to bite.

Notes on the Man Lily

On the Island where I grew up, the past must be sung into existence. Otherwise one's years will vanish like the cars on a train and never return.

On the first day of a new year, the Island's holy singer known as the Man Lily, struggles to hit the highest notes in his range.

According to tradition, the Man Lily is known for the purity of his voice and the high notes he can sing which reflect the perfection of his soul and inspire recognition of the divine.

But a Man Lily's voice tires over time. If he sings for too many audiences or too many years, he will be unable to bring the past back to life. People will die thinking their lives were meaningless.

In recent years search parties have been sent out to comb the Island and find a new Man Lily, or any male singer who can sing two Fs above middle C. Although rumors of young male tenors have been reported, no promising voices have been found.

While some Islanders suggest that this lack is due to a failing in the search, others see it as a demise of the spirit. An inability to sing the higher notes reflects the inability of our Islanders to attain nirvana.

No one wants to admit that the Island insects, or thups, are not biting the boys. Thup bites, after all, are the source of the highest notes. But Island mothers have been secretly coating their boys with pesticides and keeping them behind closed doors, long before the thups arrive in June.

While everyone loves a Man Lily, no one wants to be one. A Man Lily never marries or has offspring. He lives alone in a cave on the shore where the sick and the elderly seek his song to soothe their aching souls and bodies. Because he cannot speak, he cannot offer unwelcome advice. Instead he simply sings until followers feel the peace of his angelic song in their bones.

A happy soul, Islanders believe, hovers like a musical note above the body, or lingers just behind, like an untethered balloon.

Some souls break loose from the body when the Man Lily sings his highest notes. They become like golden Cupids floating in the pale blue of a Baroque painting. They feel such peace as they remember each year of their life as if it were a line in his song. The lucky become at one with the tune, achieving heaven without ever needing to die.

If they wish, it is said, they can return on the Man Lily's notes as well, but few ever do. To die once in the Man Lily's song is death enough for most.

These days no one knows when the Man Lily will sing his last note, or if a new Man Lily will ever be found.

Why did you leave?

people ask when I tell them of my Island past. I don't like to tell how I became so depressed, I was but a shell of a man in the end. How I didn't like anything then, not even the women or dogs. I lived alone in Costa del Sol, a town by the sea, where women went by names other than Angelina. I never spoke to anyone, not even my neighbors, two spinsters who tried to say hello day after day, week after week, as Island women will. *Trying to be friendly,* they called it as they peered into my windows at night, watching me cook and clean, reporting that I never used the phone. I never wrote letters, either, not even to my mother, but the postwoman, a terrible gossip, reported to everyone that my mother wrote me every week. I rarely went out, even for groceries, and I never ate at the local bistro, The Maria Adoncia, run by two women from Spain, and I never bought flowers from the local florist, Isabella, who had her eye on me and always hoped I'd stop in. (She once left a bouquet of roses on my doorstep with a note and her phone number tucked inside.) I never paraded through the town with the other beautiful men, as was customary during the Island holidays, and I never went to church to worship the Island God. I never worked, and I never paid taxes or voted in elections in which, of course, all the candidates were women. One day I was interviewed by a local reporter as *the man who would not vote,* and I said it wasn't a gender issue. I had no problem with women running the Island. But I didn't think they needed my vote. I don't think anyone did.

Why God Is a Woman

Last night I had a dream that you were coming to visit me by bus. I could see the waves rising against the side of the bus as you crossed the sea, and I saw your face perfectly framed in each of the bus windows. I waved and waved and called your name, *Angelina*. You never saw me, of course, but when you stepped onto the shore, you were wearing a red skirt that floated above your knees and matching buckle shoes. Mary Sues you called them. The women on the Island always name their shoes. You were smiling and talking to everyone in your Island dialect, and because you were so young and pretty, men carried your bags and showed you our town, pointing out the castles, the fort, the moss-covered homes. I remember how light your step was, how light you felt in my arms. We were kites caught in a puff of wind. But when I came close enough to see you in my dream, you were no longer you, but were your daughter instead. She looks exactly like you, Angelina. I recognized her face from a Christmas card you sent. Suddenly I remembered how many years have passed, how pathetic I am, still reaching back in time for your hands.

How did this happen? I want to ask. How did we hold each other so close once and never again, and yet I keep missing you like this? How did I turn into an old man, still telling you my life, conversing with you in my mind? Did I tell you about my neighbor who drowned in a storm last week? How the gushing river washed out the roads and broke open his house? The people saw his bed racing down the river while he snored. He was so deaf, so blind, he must have thought he was only dreaming. Maybe that's what we are all doing. Dreaming until we dream no more. Talking to no one but ourselves. When I was a boy, did I already tell you this? I had an ongoing conversation with God. I spoke to God loudly at the end of each day, complaining about the women who ran my life: my sisters, my mother, my aunt. One day my mother told me that God is a woman. She said someday I would understand.

Acknowledgments

Many thanks to the editors of the following print and online journals in which poems from this collection were first published:

Barn Owl Review, Black Scat Review, Black Tongue Review, Borderlands, Cascadia Subduction Zone, Conte, Crab Creek Review, Diagram, DMQ, Drunken Boat, The Green Door, Harpur Palate, Jenny, Knockout, La Petite Zine, Leveller, MiPoesias, Nano Fiction, NPR's 3 Minute Fiction, Plume, Poetry International, Paterson Literary Review, Poets/Artists, Praxilla, Rhino, Sweet, Quiddity.

Several of the poems also appeared in an electronic chapbook, *The Circus of Lost Dreams*, illustrated by Emily Lisker and published by Didi Menendez, 2013, available on iBooks and iTunes.

I would also like to thank Peter Conners for believing in this book; Claire Bateman and Stephanie Strickland for their insights and editorial support; my workshop friends, Karen Schubert, Erika Lutzner, Kate Lutzner, Kathleen McGookey, Sammy Greenspan, Rick Bursky, Shivani Mehta, Christopher Shipman, and Leah Umansky for their tireless readings and critiques of the poems; and my husband, Jim, and my children, Suzanne and Jimmy, for everything.

About the Author

Nin Andrews' poems and stories have appeared in many literary journals and anthologies including *Ploughshares, The Paris Review, Best American Poetry (1997, 2001, 2003, 2013), The KGB Bar Book of Poems, No Boundaries, Sudden Stories: A Mammoth Anthology of Miniscule Fiction, The House of Your Dreams: An International Collection of Prose Poems, Great American Prose Poems,* and the forthcoming anthology *Nothing to Declare: A Guide to the Flash Sequence.* The recipient of an individual artist grant from the Ohio Arts Council in 1997 and again in 2003, she is the author of six chapbooks and five full-length poetry collections. She is the mother of two grown children, and she lives in Poland, Ohio, with her husband, a physics professor and bass player, and her two Boston terriers, Sadie and Froda.

BOA Editions, Ltd. American Poets Continuum Series

Colophon

BOA Editions, Ltd., a not-for-profit publisher of poetry and other literary works, fosters readership and appreciation of contemporary literature. By identifying, cultivating, and publishing both new and established poets and selecting authors of unique literary talent, BOA brings high-quality literature to the public. Support for this effort comes from the sale of its publications, grant funding, and private donations.

❧

The publication of this book is made possible, in part, by the special support of the following individuals:

Anonymous x 2
Bernadette Catalana, *in memory of Richard Calabrese*
Gwen & Gary Conners
Anne C. Coon & Craig J. Zicari
Jonathan Everitt
Geffrey Davis
Michael Hall
William B. Hauser
Grant Holcomb
Edith Matthai, *in memory of Peter Hursh*
Boo Poulin
Deborah Ronnen & Sherman Levey
Steven O. Russell & Phyllis Rifkin-Russell
David W. Ryon